THRIVING
IN THE
TENNIS BUSINESS

SIMPLE STEPS TO SUCCEED IN THE SPORT

TRACKE
ENJOY
BOOK

THRIVING IN THE TENNIS BUSINESS

SIMPLE STEPS TO SUCCEED IN THE SPORT

A GUIDE BY SCOTT SMITH

Red Chameleon Books

Phoenix, AZ

Thriving in the Tennis Business

Copyright © 2018

All rights reserved by Scott Smith

Red Chameleon Books

Please visit www.scottsmithtennis.com

And online booksellers

Cover art by: Eduardo Cerviño
Interior page composition by Charity Walton of Good Shepherd Publications.

ISBN-13: 978-1721847266

ISBN-10:172184726X

Acknowledgements

I want to thank:

Les

Eduardo

Karen

Monetta

Randy

Brett

Clarence

Dedication

In memory of my mother,
Mona Crystal Sudders Smith Dardanis

She offered to all who knew her
smooth kindness.
She was loving, smart, and fun

Foreword

THE TENNIS BUSINESS has many aspects to it, from trying to be a top 10 ATP/WTA pro worth millions of dollars, to teaching lessons at a public park. If you love the game of tennis, it is possible to make a living and be successful in the business even if you did not make the pro tour.

Scott's years of experience has helped my transition from my professional career into the teaching/coaching industry which requires a lot of different skill sets. Promoting oneself is huge because no one else will do it for you. Organizing group lessons with many different drills so no one gets bored is challenging. Clinics and running tournaments are all ways to make money on the tennis court.

For 30+ years of Scott's knowledge, both success and failures are in this book to help any tennis lover who wants to have fun, help others, prosper in the tennis business, and skip some of the pitfalls he went through.

Brett Hansen-Dent

Preface

A COMPREHENSIVE BOOK for anyone interested in tennis or wants to learn more about the tennis business.

If you love the game and want to make a career out of the sport, this book will help you fulfill your dream.

This is my 45th year coaching tennis. Coached NAIA and NCAA Division 1 college tennis and at the high school level. Served as a USTA tournament director for both adults and juniors. Sectional singles rankings for 30 years in a row.

I've worked in all aspects of the tennis business. Much has changed over those 45 years. I've enjoyed it every day. Tennis has been my life's quest. There has never been a day I've questioned my passion.

I want to share with you my story. I have a lot to share and I think you will enjoy it.

The smile and happiness on my students' face playing tennis improved their physical ability and power of concentration. This is my most cherished reward.

The game still is simple: hit the ball over the net.

www.scottsmithtennis.com

Contents

Chapter 1

Where to Start Your Career

Passion for the Game

HOW TO START your career in the tennis business comes with some simple words: **Passion for the game.** If you have passion for what you love, it will come across as the most important thing in your life.

The first time I played tennis I was 19. I played golf as a kid growing up. Didn't learn about tennis growing up other than watching Wimbledon and the US Open. This was back with Rod Laver, John Newcombe, and Ken Rosewall among others.

I was just out of high school working in a paper mill. I was trying to go to college and working full time—difficult at 19. I was on my own.

Two courts were two blocks away from my apartment. A friend and I gave this tennis a try. The first time I played, I was hooked. This was all I wanted to do, day and night. I took two private lessons. The cost of $15 per half-hour lesson seemed like a lot of money. I still use those tips from my first teacher.

An older fellow and I played every day. He was

1

45 years old, which I thought was ancient. Not so much anymore. We used to play as much as possible while working at the paper mill. I saved up enough money for six months to stop working for the summer. I wanted to play tennis every day.

I budgeted down to the dollar what I could afford. I had to go to the unemployment office to sign up. After 10 weeks I could get unemployment benefits even though I would quit my job at the paper mill.

The woman at the unemployment office helped me and said, "I know you."

"You do?" I said.

"You play tennis," she said, "with my husband every day."

I nodded.

She continued, "I'm so grateful to you playing with him every day because he's fighting depression."

Remember, in 1972 we had little information about depression. I had never heard of depression back then.

She went on, "He takes medication for his depression and he doesn't want to leave the house unless he plays tennis with you."

During the time I spent with him, I learned so much from this man. He was a superb player and he was eager to share with me his thoughts about the game. He was a real historian of the game.

Then here it comes. The woman from the unemployment agency said, "I won't make you wait 10 weeks for your unemployment benefits. You'll receive them in a week because I want you to keep my husband active."

I'm thinking that I would play with him, anyway.

Now I'm getting paid early on my unemployment benefits to play tennis. I did notice the man deteriorate with his skills and behavior and found it difficult to watch. Mental health has always been an interesting topic for me. This is a story I'll always remember.

My family was athletic, even though I never met my father. I met an uncle, my father's brother, at his age of 65. He was athletic. No one else in my family played tennis or had any interest in it.

My aunt had a can of tennis balls when I was 10 years old. You would use the key to open the can of tennis balls in its metal container. Always thought the smell of the new balls was nothing like I'd ever smelled before. We had no racquets around the house or courts nearby.

It was a total long shot I found tennis.

Learning Your Craft from Others

I love playing blues guitar, but I've learned everything from original blues guys. Same in tennis—take ideas from each pro. Many pros will let you view a lesson or two. When I started there were older pros who helped mentor me. Those days are over. Perhaps the older pros feel threatened by the young ones taking their job away.

The older pros mentored me. I'm grateful. Without their guidance my tennis career would never have happened. They were generous with their time sharing every bit of advice with me.

I remember growing up in Denver where my mentor took me to a Denver Rockets basketball

3

game. Yes, they were the Rockets before they became the Nuggets. Before the game we saw something I'd never expected. The Australian greats John Newcombe and Ken Rosewall played a tennis exhibition.

I'd seen tennis on TV often but it was the first time I would see a pro tennis match live, thanks to my mentor. I'll never forget that night and I'll be always grateful. That instilled in me the desire to help other pros who were younger than me. I'll try to pass this forward to others.

Trust

The most important thing is to build trust with your students. You're there to help them.

Years ago I attended a workshop where the speaker said, "We're in the service business. We're there to serve our clients and not serve ourselves."

Think about that. Serve them, or yourself? Sometimes it's 50/50. We have to give a 100% of our attention to our students.

Early Experiences

My first experience teaching a tennis class began for a parks and recreation back in 1975. It was a gymnasium with a net in the middle of the basketball court and no lines for a tennis court. Basketball hoops hung where the baseline would be. A fast wood floor, 6 students, and I'm 23 years old. Perfect! I did not understand what I was doing.

Somehow, I made it work by having two people pick up balls and two people tossing, and two people hitting. It worked out well. I was so proud of myself. That experience helped me in so many instances later.

Here's another memory. I was teaching a group lesson and there's always one kid who can be a problem. He was a troublemaker. I'll get back to him soon. Remember, one third of your class loves you and one third of the class isn't sure. The middle third I would worry about.

With this kid he could influence the group in the middle, which could turn against me. So here is what happened.

Between courts sometimes there's a half-fence that stops balls from rolling into the next court. He was going for a ball and ran straight into the fence post. He went down like a domino. I thought he was dead. He stood up staggering like a pet coming off medication. About that time the class was ending and his mother came to pick him up. He already had a knot on his forehead. I apologized to his mother.

She said, "Don't worry. That should slow him down."

I couldn't believe it. I thought she would kill me!

I've also had interesting comments from students I'd like to share. I asked a woman I had in a class once if she could practice. She explained in response that she could not play during the day as she is allergic to the sun. Tennis might not be the right sport for her.

Here's another one. I taught these group lessons for an aerospace company which included a guy who had emblazoned his name on the Mars rover. I asked the class if anyone had practiced and that guy, a real rocket scientist, replied, "We're supposed to?"

One more example with the same bunch. I asked yet another class if anyone had practiced between lessons. His answer was, "Why would I do that? I'll just pick up bad habits." What can you say to that?

I taught many early lessons through parks and recreation and I'm still teaching parks and recreation classes now. They are rewarding. This is the real grass-roots of learning tennis for the local communities.

I've seen many stories with these classes and I'm experiencing one right now. Today we had a 74-year-old man and an 8-year-old boy playing with green dot junior balls. This was a sight to see.

Remember back in the early 1970s there weren't any short racquets, red and yellow balls, or green dot balls. No small nets. Very few junior racquets. We played with regular 27-inch racquets and regular balls.

It would be difficult to keep kids interested these days with all the distractions of video games

Pros Today and Kids

Pros today have it so much better than when I started. Equipment is better and YouTube videos have a good deal of tennis lessons available online. Plus, many teaching DVDs that are available.

One thing remains the same, though, after all these years: These students are trying to learn a new sport. We're there to help them.

Kids today are a little different. So many play video games. They have little patience for anything they can't do well in five minutes. I get calls from many parents asking about tennis lessons. They've never tried tennis before or know anything about it.

But the common theme from parents is, "I want my kids to do something. If tennis doesn't work out, we'll find another sport."

Some parents couldn't care less if they can play the sport well. They want their kids to be active. Many kids today have never played catch of any kind. Their hand-eye coordination is not always superb. Maybe they play soccer because it's an inexpensive team sport as we've lost many tennis players to soccer.

I have a camp I'm doing right now. Many kids have never caught a ball. When they see the ball, they close their eyes because they're scared. This class is one of the hardest I've ever had. Be familiar with it, it's the wave of the future. Parents do not work with their kids as much as before.

It's a difficult balance being a coach and a parent. I'm not sure physical activity is as important as it once was. Many schools don't have physical education classes that are mandatory, which is remarkable.

Another situation that happened many years ago while I was playing doubles on a Sunday morning. My doubles partner and I were great friends.

We played doubles tournaments together. Something wasn't right. This day my friend was out of sorts. He never had a temper, but this day was different. To my surprise, he threw his racquet, but I was standing right behind him. His racquet hit me in the nose—blood everywhere—on my shirt and the court.

I was in shock. I'm off to the emergency room. This happened in Denver, and three hospitals were placed together: The VA Denver Hospital, University of Colorado Hospital, and Rose Memorial Hospital. I walked into the VA with blood dripping everywhere. I asked the person at the desk if I could get this blood to stop.

The fellow said I had to fill out papers. I said I would love to do that but asked if they could stop the bleeding first. Again, he asked for my veteran paperwork. In my fuzzy thought process, I finally asked where I was. Then I found out that I was at the VA Denver Hospital.

My goodness, I was in the wrong hospital. So now I'm off to Rose Memorial. While in their emergency room, they took me right in and put a mask with a small hole over the nose for applying stitches. To be kind to me, they didn't want me to see the needle to numb my nose for stitches. Thirty minutes later I had five stitches.

I was married at the time and when I went home my wife asked, "What happened? You look like Frankenstein." Nice welcome home! Perhaps that explains my divorce a few years later.

The next day I was back to work at the club as an assistant pro. When the head pro looked at me he was shocked because of what had happened. Something good came from this. We told all our kids that if any players were to throw their racquet, they would be eliminated from the program. They were scared when I looked at them.

A week later I had the stitches out. Then the doctor quipped that if I did't like the way my nose looked there was always plastic surgery. Nice!

Another memory from coaching women's Division 1 College tennis. We had a talented unbelievable player from Russia. She had some of the best hands I've ever seen at the net, and her volleys were incredible. Besides that, she had a temper and a sailor's mouth. Some words in English were amazing with her Russian accent making the words unique to hear.

She was playing a singles match and received a verbal warning from the USTA umpire. The first is a warning and the next one is a point penalty. On match point down, she lost the match and went nuts. She hit a ball over the fence and into the swimming pool.

The umpire said, "I gave you a warning last time. Now it's a point penalty."

She responded, "You can't give me a (blank) point penalty." You can fill in the adjective. "I lost the match—you can't penalize me."

"Okay," the umpire said. "I'll give your teammate who's playing next to you a point penalty."

He did just that. It was a set point for her teammates opponent. The score was 5-4 40-30 and she needed one point to win the set. Umpire said, "Point for you."

The girl responded, "Great. It's set point. Now I've won the set."

The girl on our team lost the set without even playing set point. That look on her face was priceless. She said, "How did I lose the point. I never even played it?"

She was not happy with the outcome. If that's not enough drama, the two girls on our team were doubles partners. They didn't talk for a week!

Notes

Chapter 2
How to Be Professional

Tennis Professional

HOW DO WE start our journey in the tennis profession? Do you want to teach, or do you to want to play? They sound similar, but they're not. Some pros can do both, but few can do both well.

I've been successful, to a point. It's important to do both teaching and playing. Then, you can to relate what the player is feeling because you've also experienced it. Students also like to see that their coach is still competing in tournaments.

As time goes on, most coaches stop playing. Remember when you cancel a lesson to go play a tournament? It's like a doctor saying to you, "I'll play golf today and reschedule you later."

That is not the greatest feeling if you are a student trying to improve. It's important to find your priorities. Have you been around someone who has taught a lesson to you, or was your knowledge gleaned from books or YouTube? It's important to view as many lessons with other pros as possible. That's where you learn your craft, borrowing other ideas.

Ethics

When I started in the business years ago, I learned quickly. If a player approached other pros about lessons, the pros would work together with one another. I was friendly with most pros. If my student made a call or another contact, that pro would give me a courtesy call about that student. Respect had been standard years ago.

Those days are long gone. It's like the Wild West as anything goes. Many pros have said they worked with all the best players, but that is not true. It gives all pros a bad name. Some pros have an ego that is too much to handle.

Why are some pros insecure about their players? I may have the answer. Pros think their way is the only way to teach. They are also the pros who may speak ill of other pros. I stay away from them. Your results speak for themselves.

Let's establish a relationship with that pro. For example, both pros have tournaments close together with the calendar dates. If you're smart, you'll work together by saying if you play both tournaments that would reduce the price $5-$10 off your entries. This is a win. You're getting along with the other pro for future events, plus now there is a player in both tournaments.

It's important to get along in this business and not burn any bridges. Put your ego aside and invest to grow your business.

Return Phone Calls

This is easy: Return phone calls and emails within 24 hours. With most pros you'll be lucky if you hear from them soon. Many pros may be good on the court, but their business skills are lacking as well as their common sense. They register most lessons online through a club.

Take five minutes and call the student to thank him or her for signing up for the class. You won't believe how much that will help you.

Reach out to students to discuss their expectations of that class. Explain the level of the class. The class may be full or may have one student whose level may not be good enough. Sometimes people won't join a class unless a friend has signed up. If possible, the pro could create a new class for a them.

Common sense goes a long way.

Famous Pro Court Dimensions

A fellow teaching pro, a friend of mine, went to a famous pro in La Costa California. The pro was a famous world class pro and former player on the tour. My friend wanted to experience what a $100 lesson was like. Remember, my friend was a teaching pro like myself.

The first question this famous pro asked, "What are the dimensions of a tennis court?" He asked every measurement of the court. My friend wasn't sure what the dimensions were. The famous pro said, "You call yourself a tennis pro and you're not sure what the dimensions are of a tennis court?"

I didn't know the dimensions, either—I do now. I'm sure 95% of pros today do not understand what the dimensions are. Learn every angle and every dimension of the court if possible. If you ever want to find out a pro's knowledge, ask him the dimensions of the court.

Physical Demands

A tennis professional routinely spends 5-7 hours a day on the tennis court, in the hot sun. A long day on the court can be brutal and exhausting, tough on skin, joints, eyes, etc.

After hours on the court, the pro will answer phone calls, emails, and texts. This is not to mention meetings with staff and the general manager. Then, the public, who is always right.

When you make a full-time career decision to be a tennis professional, most people think you play tennis all day. Furthest thing from the truth.

Tennis facilities may not provide an independent contractor with health insurance or a retirement program such as a 401K.

Volunteer Your Time

I've been asked to be on many USTA grievance committees. These are usually adult leagues accusing others of cheating and bending the rules. At times, it has to do with self-rating described by players. I've served on about 9 or 10 committees during the years. People's behavior never ceases to amaze me.

My advice is to volunteer for these committees as much as possible. You'll meet great contacts with those from the USTA. You may find this networking can benefit you, such as opportunities in gaining USTA Junior or Adult tournaments.

I've been on Community and Advocacy committees. Volunteer situations can take up a lot of time. Nevertheless, I recommend doing it.

Physical Appearance

Physical appearance is important. You're a role model of fitness for your students. Young children and parents want to see you as the picture of health.

Clean clothes are a must. Remember you're the role model. Shoe bottoms rarely wear out and are made much better than 30 years ago. Years ago, a product like epoxy for holes in shoes was available. I don't think they make this product anymore. I've found that putting your shoes in the washing machine is a quick fix. Besides, your shoes appear much cleaner.

Pressed shirts and shorts are a must for that first impression. Racquet bags with demo racquets are important to have on the court. How many times have your students forgotten their racquets? Or the racquets found another car the wife or husband used that day? I hear, "My bag is in my husband's car as we had to switch cars today." Or, "My kids used it today for a high school match."

It's common sense to have extra racquets available. This can be helpful especially if a pro shop is affiliated with a club or a tennis store nearby for sales.

Most pros may know about Roger Federer, Serena Williams, and current pro events. Learn everything outside this to set yourself apart from the others. Is it possible to go on a field trip to a pro or college event? It's easy to find out about the local high school teams and college teams in your area. Many major cities have junior college tennis teams.

I did clinics in the Lake Arrowhead area with Dennis Ralston and Oscar Wegner. We had many participants attend both events. We had close to

75 people at each event. Both are unique and have different views in their approaches to tennis. They both had many opinions about the game.

I was part of another clinic when six local pros came together from local area clubs. We had six pros and six courts with each of us doing our favorite drills on our court. During the week, we as pros were competitors with each other having our own programs.

This day we were there for our drills and it was awesome. We switched courts every 20 minutes for the 2-hour clinic. We had companies donating hit for prizes. We charged $10 per player.

Anyone can put this together. We had a group picture at the end that I still have today.

Chapter 3

High School Coach, USPTA, PTR, and Insurance

More Knowledge

WHERE DOES A high school coach gain more knowledge of coaching? The coaches hope to expand tennis programs but may not be sure how to improve them.

Does that help to be a good college player? Yes, it does. Most high school coaches are not ex-college players. Most high school coaches teach math, English, and other subjects. How does one become a good high school coach?

Consider joining the USPTA or PTR. I've been an USPTA member for over 30 years. Many great high school workshops are helpful. Some incorporate drills, managing a team, etc., and both organizations come with insurance.

Often, clubs and public facilities won't hire a pro without a pro being a member of the USPTA-PTR. The main reason is insurance. Becoming a member of these organizations doesn't make a pro a good high school coach, but it can help.

California Interscholastic Federation (CIF) has

clinics for high school coaches. There are USTA high school workshops available.

My suggestion is to watch a top team's practice if possible. Watch coaches at league playoffs and individual tournaments. Many league tournaments are free to the public to watch and great tournaments come to mind. The Ojai Tournament in California is terrific!

Most coaches are friendly when you ask them questions. Some find it flattering. Many successful high school coaches are also teaching pros at clubs and parks. If you were to take a lesson, I'm sure they would help answer questions. Most coaches want to share their secrets of success.

Stipends for High School Coaches

Let's talk about a stipend for high school coaches. In California, the average is $3,000 per season. That could fluctuate at some private schools. Making the playoffs adds 10% to the stipend per week after your season ends.

So, another $300 per week if you're in the playoff tournament. If a player takes part in individuals, that adds another 5% to your stipend per week, or around $150 per week. Not a lot.

Some schools don't pay coaches if they go to the playoffs. Most of those schools are private schools. Public schools, by law, must pay upon reaching the playoffs.

Other states compensate more but sometimes their season is shorter. It depends on the school district and state. Most schools will do a complete background check which is important for a school district.

I work at a private Catholic high school which

is extraordinarily strict by the Archdioceses. Public high schools post their tennis job within the school. The faculty is first choice to fill these positions. If no teachers are interested, a person outside the school might be hired.

Several friends are pros who have coached in a public school. The school must post the tennis position to the teachers currently on faculty staff. Occasionally, pros lose those positions. Some friends who are independent contractors have lost their job to a staff faculty member.

USPTA Certification

Let me tell you about me taking my USPTA certification test in 1978 at the Denver Country Club. When I took my test, I needed a recommendation letter from a current USPTA member. That member wrote a letter saying, in essence, "Why would you be an asset to the organization?"

The head pro at the club where I was working, was kind enough to write a nice recommendation letter for me. This was when ball colors were changing from white to "Optic Yellow." I'm not sure what Optic Yellow is, except it's easier to see.

Anyway, the balls were different. Some were two-tone yellow and green balls like the red and yellow balls today. They also had purple balls. Yes, purple balls. The pro at the club had a teaching basket with purple balls. These were the balls I took my skills test with. I'd never seen a purple tennis ball before. It terrified me!

The skills test went well. Then came the private and group lessons. This USPTA certification test was on a Sunday afternoon. The tester needed students for my private and group lesson. What better students for a lesson than a family swimming at the pool! We had a family of four—mother, father, sister, and brother were doing the head pro a favor by helping with this test.

The sister and brother wanted no part of this. They wanted to stay at the pool with their friends. Instead, they were on the court dripping water as they walked through the gate. I'm sure they didn't wear tennis shoes, just flip flops.

The group lesson is 20 minutes on the backhand. Let me recap a family straight out of the pool: Soaking wet, no shoes, and purple balls, and I was 25 years old! It's all good, right? The mother and father were sympathetic and kind to my needs. The brother and sister wanted to go back and jump off the high dive.

Next came the private lesson after the group lesson which should be a walk in the park. This lesson was on the serve. I talked about the difference between serving with backhand and continental grip.

The student had a question for everything I said to him. I was happy to answer him to the best of my ability. I thought it went well. Remember, still using purple balls and the family soaking wet from the swimming pool. I was ready for this day to end!

The tester sent back the results and you had to wait for the USPTA to mail the results. The mail came with the results. I had tested P1 level on everything except the group lesson. That brought my overall rating down to P2. Imagine that for a group lesson with the family from the swimming pool and purple balls.

P1 is what is called an Elite Pro now. This is the highest rating other than a master pro.

USPTA Upgrade Paul Xantos

Years later, I upgraded the group lesson to P1, Elite Pro. Paul Xantos did my upgrade. If you know any history about the USPTA, you would be aware of Paul Xantos. He helped write the *USPTA Tennis A Professional Guide 1984*. I recommend it if you haven't read it.

I ran into Paul a few times at some Wilson events. He always said he would give me an upgrade. I was coaching an NAIA college women's team and we had a match with Pierce College. Our match was before the men's match.

Paul was the coach of the men's team at Pierce College. He had an incredible winning record. We had finished the women's match. The men's match was about to start. It was spring break.

I asked Paul if he was ready to do the upgrade with the group lesson.

One of the players said, "Coach, where's the other team? Isn't the men's team supposed to play?"

More players kept asking and Paul was getting frustrated. The team he was supposed to play never showed up.

In addition, I was bothering him about the upgrade. Steam was coming out of his ears. It scared me to death because he was such a legend and a larger-than-life personality.

He finally gave up on the match and let his players leave. Once again, it was spring break.

Now it was time for my upgrade. Here we go again with a crazy group lesson. He found four people playing frisbee to take a 20-minute lesson again on the backhand. The backhand again 10 years later. I explained the grips and then hit balls.

21

After it was over, Paul said, "You know what you're doing but you did it all wrong. You need to watch them hit first and then correct the mistakes."

I may have disagreed, but at that stage I just asked, "Did I pass?"

He said, "You passed!"

I felt like I got a blessing from the Pope. There will never be another Paul Xantos. I'm grateful that I became friends with him.

I would also like to mention another legend in Southern California, Pete Brown. I could write a book on what he meant to me and to the tennis world. He was the most giving and generous man I ever met in tennis. He did so much for underprivileged kids in Southern California. I'm sure there are scholarships in his name.

Learn from these legends and give back to the game!

I was fortunate to receive the USPTA District 5 Pro of the Year in 2013 in Southern California. I did a lot of volunteer work for underprivileged kids and they recognized me for my work. It was a nice accolade to receive.

My advice to any new pro starting out: Volunteer for as many committees and free clinics as you can. People put a name to your face. You'll get back so much more in return!

Other Mentors

Two other mentors helped me—Bob Parker and Jeff Abby.

Bob Parker was quite a character, a few pounds

to the good. A cowboy hat was his fixture. He smoked cigarettes while giving lessons. Never stopped feeding balls with a cigarette in his mouth like Keith Richards playing guitar.

It wasn't the best look for a tennis pro. His appearance stood out, and that's a fair statement. But he was the nicest man one could ever meet. He cared and tried to help mentor other pros.

He bought my first stringing machine. I wish I'd never sold it to him. I've since bought another one like that. The lesson here is: Don't judge a book by its cover. I learned a lot from him.

Jeff Abby was another original. A member receives a number when they join the USPTA. The numbers are usually assigned in order when a member joined the organization. Jeff's USPTA member was #11. I'm sure the first 10 members had passed away.

People loved him, and he had quite a following for years. His students didn't care if they improved, they just wanted to be around Jeff, including me. I learned from him his kindness and professionalism with his students. He would arrive for lessons an hour early and wait on the court for his lesson to start.

One time I needed advice. I relied on Jeff for his genuine friendship and common sense. I asked him for his advice and he said, "I give my best sitting down."

We sat down on the bench on the court and he gave me advice as only Jeff could do.

In 2002 I wanted to do something special for him. A friend at the time was president of the USPTA. I told him about Jeff and I wanted to get him the recognition he deserved.

The president sent Jeff a plaque that recognized his service to the tennis community. The best part was the day of this recognition. He didn't know what was about to happen. It was at noon Saturday when both of our lessons finished. We taught right next to each other. I knew most his students and I could inform them about the award.

At around 11:45 AM, Jeff was ending his lesson early, but his students knew they wanted to stay till noon. His students kept saying, "Let's hit more overheads and volleys."

About 11:55 AM, people walked on the court. By noon, around 30 people gathered with him.

The look on his face was priceless. I'm glad I helped put this event together. He was touched and humbled by this. Jeff deserved everything that people said about him.

Volunteer Assistant

A volunteer assistant can be a good way to get your foot in the door with coaching. You can learn from the head coach and be hired as an assistant in a small capacity. You may volunteer for a summer camp.

Assisting with fundraising. Coaches always want help with fundraising. It's a year-round project that never ends. E-mails, and phone calls, texts, etc., can overwhelm most coaches. A volunteer assistant can help.

A volunteer assistant can be a former college player looking to get in the coaching ranks. Sometimes a father who was a good player tries to help with his child's team. Former players can scout future opponents, read statistics charts, etc. The volunteer assistant can help drive to locations of matches.

Many volunteer assistants want to be with a winning program. I've seen many volunteer coaches who will work for free to be around a successful team.

I'm not sure where you draw the line from working to free. I love this sport like no other but working free for a winning program just to say you're with a winning team—I don't understand it.

Here is a tip that will help you if you're at a school or a park. Make sure you have access to the courts. There isn't a worse feeling than not having keys to open the courts. You look foolish!

Some schools have difficulty in communication with union janitor maintenance workers. It's so important to have a good relationship with an athletic director or park director. Even before opening the courts, make sure the parking lot and gates are open. This can be a real headache.

NOTES

Chapter 4
Good Players Become Good Pros

Former ATP Pros

CAN SOME GOOD players become good pros? Absolutely. But not all. Former ATP tour and college players can relate to what a player is feeling in a match situation.

The best lesson I ever saw was a former No. 6 in the world with a basket and six balls in it. I won't say who the pro was, but he didn't miss a ball. It was incredible to watch. The student was a male 3.0 player.

Players' Reputation

Some pros live on their reputation. Often, you'll see a bio of a former ATP player. I was close to getting a point in doubles on the ATP tour. Does that make me a former ATP pro? No, but pros exaggerate all the time.

I used to work as a feeder at a club in Southern California. One of the greatest players of all time was there when he was 13 or 14. I fed him balls in the workouts. Does that make me his coach? Of course not. Some pros would say they were his coach which is disgusting!

Some children are playing and their parents are big names in tennis. Southern California is a hotbed for great players. I've known many. A year ago I lost a close friend whose son is now on the tour—top 50 in the world. This is a lot of pressure for the young players.

Coaching situations can become awkward for some parents and players. That's because of the parents playing background. It's a nice problem to have. Many of these players participate in college tennis at major schools.

When I coached college tennis, I knew a few so-called big-name parents. Some of them didn't come around much to watch, which I thought was strange. Maybe the parents don't want to let go of the past?

Tennis Academies

What is an academy? It sounds like a fancy name for a school. Some academies in Southern California seems to pop up on every corner. The word "Academy" is etched in parents' minds. I'm not sure they could tell you what an academy is.

An academy is like a boarding school, where students live and go to school. There are pros here who have an academy, but the players don't practice until after school. That's called a tennis workout.

Numerous major academies are held in Florida and California. If a student take lessons in the afternoon at the academy, does that mean he or she is in the academy? How can you advertise it as an "Academy" if no people board at the facility?

This indicates the vague part of the word, "Academy." It's an important phrase that most, including me, don't understand.

Playing Tournaments

I've been fortunate to have played senior tennis in Southern California for the past 30 years. I've had 30 years of consecutive SCTA USTA singles rankings, starting in men's 35 singles. I finished playing in the men's 60 singles. Now I'm eligible for the men's 65 singles. I estimate I played roughly 260 tournaments in 30 years. I'm proud of this record. I've played everywhere you can play in Southern California.

Despite the number of tournaments, many facilities have disappeared. Tennis courts in neighborhoods have not evolved as revenue makers. Some facilities in neighborhoods were alone as tennis clubs' years ago, but now are surrounded by homes, shopping centers, etc.

I could list at least 10 facilities that are gone—sign of the times. Land has become too valuable and the owners may sell out for a huge profit. It happens all the time. What is the lesson?

Public facilities and parks are not going anywhere. A club's owners can make a fortune selling the land. Some club owners say they will never sell their facilities. Money has a way of changing people's minds.

My suggestion for longevity in this business is to find a public facility.

The first tournament I played was unlike any tournament I've ever played since. They called it a "Bisque Tournament," a form of a handicapping tournament. They give players a certain amount of points per set to use at the players choice.

The tournament director viewed each player and awarded the lower players with points they could use when they saw fit. Maybe several in a set for a player. Anyway, my opponent received one Bisque Point to use whenever he wanted. The tournament was one set. Remember, this was 45 years ago. My opponent was serving at 6-5, 40-30 match point.

He then said, "I'll use my Bisque Point right now. That gave him the set and the match without playing match point."

I was thinking what happened; I lost! It was a lot of fun, and I never played another one since. It's not a bad idea, but the opinion of the tournament director was a final decision as to the level of that player.

The new fast 4 format is also a great handicapping system. This format checks off numerous boxes. Let's say you have a guy 45 years old who still thinks he's a 5.0 player, but wouldn't win in a 2 out of 3-set match with a college player. In a short format he can compete with no-add scoring. Many older players will not play a tournament to avoid playing a player in their 20's.

Women's draws are smaller in adult tournaments. I'm not sure why. Again, with this format many women could play, and it would grow significantly.

Some tournaments are now going to shorter sets. A pro set is popular now in a round robin form. Players like to know they start and finish at a certain time.

How many times have you played a tournament? For example, if a match is at 11:00 am and it's an hour drive to the event. Plus, you might warm up at 9:00 and leave at 10:00. You spend an hour just driving to the event. Once you arrive the tournament is delayed. You don't get on the court till noon even though the match is at 11:00.

You may lose or win quickly. Then another hour drive home. There goes your whole day. These quick formats end in three hours, plus playing many opponents.

Universal Tennis Rating (UTR) is the next big event that will change the entire landscape of tennis. It already happened in some areas. All the seedings for higher level junior tournaments use Universal Tennis Rating. It takes a combination of games played with a player at about your same level. It's revolutionized junior tennis.

All of Europe is using it and the ITF (International Tennis Federation). Numerous UTR tournaments now compete with the USTA junior tournaments.

When I played pro satellite tournaments in New Zealand, I saw an interesting idea about a policy of officiating matches. The policy specified that if a player lost the match, the player had to sit in the umpire's chair and officiate the next match.

This was the last thing players want to do after they lose. It made players think about sportsmanship and line calls, and how difficult being an umpire can be.

Imagine if that happened here at a sanctioned

tournament. Players would go nuts. One stipulation they made was that if you did not officiate after your loss they would ban you from playing tournaments for six months. Imagine if that was the way it is now?

I thought it was a great idea. I didn't like officiating and it made me want to work harder on my game, so I wouldn't have to officiate anymore.

An incident happened at a tournament in Pasadena. I was playing on a court that had metal nets. Have you ever played on a court with metal nets? It's the worst. When you get a let or when the ball hits the top of the net, the ball doesn't fall on the court. It takes a strange bounce. It could now become an overhead instead of a ball that lands on the court that doesn't bounce.

I was playing this guy. We were in a 9-point tie-breaker. Remember those? At 4 all it's set point for both players. Now it's 4-4 set point for me, match point for him, and the ball hits the top of the net. It turns into an overhead for me, that I could win the point and the set.

I had a few friends watching who cheered when I won the point to win the set. My opponent was going crazy. He screamed and was swearing at my friends and went to his car to get a tire iron to go after my friends.

I tanked the 3rd set. I didn't want to play but if you defaulted the match the tournament wouldn't count for a ranking, so I had to finish even though I wasn't interested. After I lost, my opponent asked me to play doubles in the next tournament. Now remember, this was a guy going after my friends with a tire iron. I declined his invitation.

I remember playing in a 35 and over singles senior tournament at the Racquet Center in Studio City. If you ever played there, you know how hot it can get! Temperature was 102 and, on the court, probably 115-120.

They sent an 85 doubles match on right next to us. On the changeover, one guy walked off the court and never came back. The other players went to look for him and they found he had left.

That brought me to my match. We had split sets and a changeover in the third set. Both of us left the court to get water at the drinking fountain. The match was competitive on both sides.

I asked him at the drinking fountain what he did for a living.

He answered, "I'm a heart doctor."

"Great," I said. "You can save me when I drop from the heat."

The doctor said, "I'll save you when the match is over."

What else can you say?

Sports Psychology

Sports psychologists have become popular in tennis and other sports in the past 25-30 years. One of the most famous ones who started this idea was also a player.

He was practicing with a friend of mine. My friend was a good player and was winning in a practice match against him. The sports psychologist was having a difficult day. He had to stop playing because he threw all his racquets over the fence and couldn't continue.

Outside the court, the weeds were 6-8 feet high with snakes and things. No one wanted to look for tennis racquets. Remember, this is the person telling you how to control your emotions!

Teaching Aids

Teaching tools and ball machines are great. Many on court targets can be purchased and put on the court like a movie prop. Students love these gimmicks.

I've used them all. I like ball machines but they're always dangerous because of a ball getting stuck in the cylinder. Players using the ball machine will try to get the balls to free up and work again. I've seen a few accidents with fingers and hands.

My advice is to make sure the user completely knows what could happen.

Fees for ball machines can be lucrative, but the machines will tear up the balls much faster. I've always used balls that had a lot of wear on them for a ball machine.

Chapter 5
Director of Tennis: Head Pro

Director of Tennis Job Description

YEARS AGO, THE top title at a club was the Head Pro. Now the main title is Director of Tennis, and the Head Pro is the next top title. Next would be Head of Junior Development. Then would be the Tennis Professional.

The director of tennis oversees all aspects of all the programs. This includes working with all the pros under the director. In addition, the director collaborates with the board and management.

Most likely, the director will have a staff meeting once a week or every other week. A meeting with management is scheduled once a week, which might include the club's members.

Primarily, the head pro teaches the most, although not always.

The tennis professional is trying to get as many lessons that the director and head pro pass up. The head of junior development works with the juniors and coordinates junior teams, tournaments, etc.

A junior coordinator schedules junior tennis matches with other clubs. The coordinator may manage junior club tournaments, USTA junior tournaments, and other items. The assistant to the junior coordinator might be a good high school or college player. This assistant might receive free lessons or minimal pay.

Racquet Contracts

Racquet contracts for pros are driven by sales. That's it, sales. Years ago, big-name racquet company's budgets were much bigger. There weren't online sales like Tennis Warehouse, Tennis Express, Midwest Sports and others, so companies were very generous with products for pros.

The quantities of racquets sold determined how much the company would support the pros. How many clubs have pro shops these days? Pro shops are dwindling down quickly.

What happens if a pro has a demo program, and a student demos a racquet they like? Three days later, the student shows up at the lesson with a new racquet. You would ask if the student has a new racquet and the student replies, "Yes, I bought it online because it was less expensive."

Okay, so let's go through the timeline. You allowed them to try your demo. They liked it but bought it from an online dealer. You've lost the sale and future perks from the rep and racquet company. This happens all the time. Pro shops are being reduced to stringing, selling some racquets, maybe some shoes.

Stringing is keeping these shops alive. Online sales are killing shops and pros. It's also not helping the sales reps that much either. I predict in 5-10 years there may not be any sales reps left, due to online sales.

The one thing that could help the pro and pro shop sales is to have a demo day. Racquet companies love demo days as long is there a retail store they're affiliated with.

Demo days are great for making revenue. Two-hour demo days are common in today's business. Most of these companies will have "FREE" things to give away for players who take part. You would make income by charging for the clinic plus them playing with all the latest racquets.

Hopefully that will generate sales. Sometimes a racquet company will be happy to send you a banner for advertising for your facility and have one of their banners on a wall or a fence. In return the company may have equipment available for the pros for free or at a reduced rate.

How to Start a Program from Scratch

Want to set up a junior program from scratch? These are ideas that I've used to be successful when trying to start a junior program at your facility.

Suppose it's a private club. The first thing I would do is to mention something in the club's newsletter. At my club, we used to have "FREE" junior lessons on Friday afternoon right before free golf lessons. Five to ten kids would come. Sure, it's free and you may never get them to come to lessons and pay. However, for every ten kids who came to a free lesson, an average of three would come too and pay for lessons.

The key is to have kids come to the lesson with a friend, brother, or sister. The majority who come alone are alone because the parents want them to come.

A good deal of players who come by themselves may not come back. It's not always a great scenario. Like any business, you must give away a few things to attract students. Once they're in your program, another incentive is a lesson plan to buy five lessons and get the sixth lesson free!

After they're in your program, players and parents become competitive and want to compete against others in their age group. That's where USTA Junior team tennis takes place. When that starts you can have a few workouts during the week after school.

What if you're at a high school or at a public facility such as a park without a newsletter? Is it possible for the school to send out an email telling the parents about your program? If you're at a park, does the city have tennis lessons? If not, maybe you could set up a program.

The tennis business is hard, especially trying to start a brand-new program. When starting an adult program you can use the same formula I described with the juniors. Once again, these are my ideas. I'm sure you've got some ideas that may work for you.

Chapter 6

Which Is Right for You: Clubs or Public Facilities and Parks?

PROS ARE HAPPY to be employed, landing a job. Public facilities are usually negotiated with a lease through a city, or it can be a park that's run through the city. City council meetings and park commission meetings are prevalent. I taught at a city facility for 25 years.

Board Members

Board members control clubs. The boards usually consist of an odd number, like 7, 9, 11. Some club board members have term limits.

I've worked at both public facilities and clubs. I feel more secure in a public facility. It's more community friendly than a closed club. Also, sometimes general managers don't last long at many clubs. If the club is struggling, it's the general manager who may be responsible and let go.

Clubs can be a popularity contest with the board members. You may have a friend on the board who is no longer on the board because of term limits or a resignation. The new board member has some-one else in mind for your position. Next thing you know you're out. Not always, but it happens.

Another story to tell about a club. While work-ing at a club, I met a young girl who was a member. She was short-changed athletically, but her deter-mination was incredible. We had a ball machine at the club but the extension cord was only about 10 feet long. At 6:00 AM, she would lug in her own 30-foot extension cord, plug it into an electric socket, and use the ball machine.

The ball machine had a heavy cover to protect it from the weather and I packed it away on top of a piece of plywood. She would have to move the ply-wood and roll out the ball machine onto the court to use it. It was awkward and heavy to move. I would come to work and there she was hitting balls. I'd seen nothing like this. She could have never done this at a public facility.

Skate Parks

A city I worked at planned to install a skate park in place of two tennis courts. I attended parks and recreation meetings but to no avail. We said peo-ple would ride their skateboards to the skatepark. City council members said, "No, that will not hap-pen. The police will give tickets to those riding their skateboards to the park."

We fought against this for a long time, but we lost. The tennis courts were demolished. The city built the skatepark.

The dedication began and on this particular evening while city council members were talking at the podium, a skateboarder rode down the hill, lost control, and fell. The skateboarder and skateboard took off like a missile.

Then the skateboarder was rolling on the ground. He wound up beneath a car's rear tires. Just at the time he was near the back tires, the car started to roll backward with this guy underneath the tires.

The car stopped, and he was okay, but the city council members couldn't believe what they had seen. It was what we told them would happen.

USTA Grants

USTA grant money is available for court renovation and resurfacing. I'm the head coach of a high school. We were awarded $4,000 for court resurfacing. It took 8 months with a little help from my school to get the grant.

The USTA doesn't make it easy and every penny was earned. Drawings, pictures, and plans are required. The gates need to be a certain distance to allow wheelchair access.

Different levels of grants are available depending on what your facility offers. For after school, weekends and future events, the USTA needs programming updates on all events. USTA required blended blue lines for younger programs.

It's possible you can receive a grant, but you'll work very hard to get one. When our facility is complete, it will be awesome.

USTA has grants for players after-school programs with hardships. I know several who have received grants. People think they can receive this with a grant writer, and possibly they can. But there are certain things you have to answer to get these. I will not go into much detail because I don't want to give out any wrong information.

Chapter 7

Tennis Workshops and Networking

IF YOU HAVE the passion for tennis, you'll want to attend workshops. Workshops are like a buffet line. They look interesting. Try it.

Years ago, I upgraded to a USPTA Elite Pro. This USPTA master pro who upgraded me would attend every available tennis workshop. He forgot more about tennis than most people would ever know. He mentioned it was worth it to learn one tip from any pro at a conference.

Now, are some of these workshops not worthwhile? Possibly. I've always enjoyed workshops with guest pros. You can always learn something from anyone.

Networking

Networking is vital to establish contacts. Tennis business is a small world. You never know who you might cross paths with.

Workshops and guest speakers are always informative. You can share tips with other pros that can be helpful. Different sections of the country have USPTA workshops and divisional meetings.

Southern California has many USPTA workshops and vendor shows.

Spanish System

The Spanish system of teaching is available in various areas of the United States. I've been to a few seminars and they are good. Spain has developed a lot of good players and so has the United States.

I worked with a player who spent last summer at an academy in Spain. It was a good experience for her to play on red clay. She saw a part of the world and experienced things she may not have experienced here, and she improved a lot.

Not much attention was paid to the volley and overheads because of the slow red clay.

I saw many of their workouts on YouTube. You can improve a lot in the United States. There are plenty of good players in the United States to play.

Too many players and parents chase ITF points in the juniors. There could be a book about the ITF.

YouTube Tennis Lessons

YouTube and internet tennis lessons are common. I was on a mailing list with internet lessons for free. Free lessons are just that, free lessons. Some were superb, and some were horrible.

A market exists with internet lessons. Many pros run ads through their internet lessons to generate income. A student of mine came to a group lesson. We had a lesson on the volleys and his volleys were decent.

I asked him where he learned how to volley. He said, "YouTube."

He had a continental grip which was remarkable. Most students swing too much on a volley. His volleys were short and compact, the way they should be. It amazed me how well he did without taking a lesson from a human.

You can find anything on YouTube. I'm not sure what makes some of these teachers credible. They don't have to be great teachers or players if someone subscribes to their YouTube channel. They're making money with all the ads they sell. Some online lessons have monthly fees for the student.

There are a few good reasons players enjoy internet lessons. Players don't have to pay as much. Some were lessons on strategy and point structures and other ideas. The biggest reason is they like YouTube lessons, they don't have to leave their house.

I've tried not to describe any teaching or lessons structure on playing points or strategy in this book. The reason is that there are many books on this topic already available.

Notes

Chapter 8

Leases Through Cities: What Are They?

Five to Ten Year Leases

LEASES ARE THROUGH cities with agreements for normally five to ten years. This can be great and horrible at the same time. For example, there is a lease through a city and there is a seven- or nine-member board. Board members change often and two or three friends who helped you get your facility may leave for another position.

The new board members may have someone else in mind, such as one of their friends. The next thing you know you've lost your facility after you've put your heart and soul into making the facility better.

You could improve windscreens, court resurfacing, upgrades and other items. It happens all the time. A lot of leases with cities have a percentage that the vender will give to the city as a monthly payment.

The best thing to do is get a 10-year lease, which are difficult to get. Tennis corporations have many public facilities and looking to gain more.

Many facilities have more pros than the availability of courts. A facility has 15 courts and they have 12 pros. That means if everyone is teaching there are only 3 courts left for the members to play on. This scenario would never happen. They hire so many pros because it's important to match the correct player with the correct coach.

Chapter 9
USTA Adult & Junior League Opportunities

Adult League Opportunities

NUMEROUS LEAGUES AND tournaments are available. USTA adult leagues are important to a facility. These teams have the potential to go all the way to the USTA National Finals.

That's a strong statement. How exciting to be part of the team that could advance to the Sectionals and qualify for the Nationals. That would make a coach look terrific and make the club look good. It's a lot of fun to get members excited to play for a National title.

This is a great way to establish a lesson base if you're willing to work at it. Some league matches play away at other clubs. Take the time and go watch your students. You'll have those students for a long time.

Same with juniors. Watch team tennis matches and they'll attend your workouts and private lessons. Do you charge them to watch them play? Probably not unless you're a huge name. The rest of us will do it for free. The rewards down the road will be substantially better.

USTA Net Generation is a relatively new program. I believe this is a good program which consists of a background check.

Junior League Opportunity

Many pros earn most of their income from Junior league opportunities. Junior team tennis is usually on the weekends. Matches are held at home and away. A match can consume a good part of the day.

The best way to receive revenue from team tennis is to promote workouts after school twice weekly, if not more. It's important to be there on the weekends for matches. That means traveling to away matches. How much income do you lose from lessons by traveling with these teams? That's a question difficult to answer.

You might send an assistant pro if you're fortunate to have one. However, to start this program you must be involved and hands-on in your team tennis. Driving back and forth to the matches requires parents' involvement.

This can come with a price. Suppose you have a parent drive to an event, but that child is not one of the stronger players. Does that player get playing time because the parent helped you drive? This is a tough question.

Remember that the other parents are watching what you do about playing time. I've heard about parents fighting with their coaches and other parents about playing time.

The best solution is to have a team meeting with all the players and parents before the season starts.

Easy to say, difficult to do. My high school team has contracts signed by both parents and players.

It sounds like this may take the fun out being a player. It's the best thing you could do. After a few years doing these you'll have experience in human behavior.

This becomes a good way for an assistant to become part of an established program of junior tennis. Learn from the head pro before you venture out on your own.

Wheelchair Tennis

Wheelchair tennis is incredible to watch. The players' strength and stamina are inspirational. They play wheelchair tennis at every Grand Slam.

Certain facilities are wheelchair friendly. The tennis gates must be a specific width to accommodate the wheelchairs. This can add tremendous value to your facility and program.

I don't know what it takes to get a Wheelchair tournament. Donating the courts for an hour or two would be a great investment in goodwill with the program. I observed Wimbledon Wheelchair finals on the grass courts.

This should send a message to tennis directors who manage the courts' facilities. If wheelchairs were abusing the courts, I'm sure the All England Club would not allow wheelchairs on the grass courts.

NOTES

Chapter 10

Tournament Directors: How to Become One

USTA Tournaments Available

THERE ARE NUMEROUS USTA tournaments held locally. The USTA requests that tournament directors have background experience in running tournaments.

One recent change requires that tournaments use an USTA referee. It can cost $180 per day. That's why it's good to find sponsors.

My recommendation is to start at the lowest level. A USTA Level 7 Junior Novice Tournament. A referee wouldn't be needed at an entry level tournament. After that it's possible to work up to higher tournaments.

Being a volunteer can be a huge assist at a big tournament. The tournament director will not say "No" to your help.

If possible, learn the USTA Tournament Data Manager (TDM). Tournament directors pay others to do the TDM work, home page, and make draws and schedules. To learn TDM is a huge bonus for you! Make that a priority. You must attend a TDM workshop to hold a tournament in Southern California.

I can't emphasize enough to learn TDM. It's so important to directors of tennis and clubs. Few pros are familiar with the format.

USTA tournaments can be lucrative. Consider charging $35 for singles and $25 per player for doubles. The USTA will charge a $3 surcharge on each member entering online. At the tournament end, there is a $1 singles fee for each player and $2 per doubles team.

Most tournaments play a tiebreaker instead of a 3rd set and this will save money because you're not using additional balls.

Securing courts to hold a tournament can be a problem. One possibility could be high school facilities. Once again, being a member of the United States Professional Tennis Association (USPTA), or the Professional Tennis Registry (PTR) could help.

Many clubs and facilities hate to give up their courts for several hours. This is a problem with USTA adult leagues and junior tennis teams. Some proceeds from a tournament can benefit the tennis program. That makes it a little easier sometimes to gain courts.

Insurance for tournaments is also difficult. The USTA offers insurance for their tournaments. We had them write a policy for a tournament that was held last year. They're somewhat secretive about this, but it exists. I've used another form of insurance through the USPTA. I'm less familiar with the PTR.

Tournament Parents

Some parents do not know how to read a draw sheet. I get calls, "Who is this family named Bye? They're everywhere in the draw." The tournament director can make life easier if it's possible to educate the parents.

I have two USTA sanctioned junior tournaments and one sanctioned adult tournament. I'm able to get sponsors to help with the cost. Selling advertising can help pay for T-shirts, trophies, balls, and other items for a tournament.

One of my tournaments was held in a mountain resort area. I contacted a motel which helped defray my costs. The hotel advertised on the homepage of my tournament which worked out well because some of players chose to stay there.

A hospice company sponsored my tournament. A hospice might not seem ideal for a tennis tournament, but it covered my cost for trophies, T-shirts, and balls. People love to help junior tournaments, if you ask. They also enjoy seeing their companies on the back of T-shirts.

Companies want to feel part of the local community. It's good public relations. We can try to have a banner up or giveaways at the tournament desk. All the company can do is say "No." It doesn't hurt to ask.

Notes

Chapter 11
Percentage of Lessons for You

Ladders, Cardio Tennis, Club Mixers, and Pickleball

Percentage of Lessons

PARKS AND RECREATION may offer 65-70% of lessons. For example, if you make $70 an hour, you're lucky if you get $45. This isn't always the case. Some big-name pros will get more than that. The Director of Tennis gets a small portion, plus some to the club.

Here is a big myth: Students think the pros will get the full price of the lesson, whether it's $60 or $70 per hour. Why am I not a tennis pro? (They're the ones making a lot of money.) Group lessons for assistant pros can be a flat rate of an estimate of $25-$45.

Ladders

Ladders are a great way to generate income. I know pros who have ladders at their club and charge their members. Ladders can be arranged online. Some have ladders outside the facility which would match up UTR ratings. You might have a 12-year-old play someone in their 50s. That would be an interesting scenario.

Universal Tennis Rating (UTR), uses a combination of games played, an opponent's ability, etc. Many tournaments use this system for seedings.

An event was called, "Youth vs Experience." For example, a top 60-year-old played a 12-year-old. A 55-year-old vs 14-year-old. All these matches were top players in each age group. You get the idea. It was fun to watch the different styles of play.

These players would have never been on the same court with the other players. Make sure your ladder matches have the rules set because players manipulate these rules. I've heard the cost of a ladder can be $30-50 for three months. It's a good revenue for the person organizing the ladder.

Cardio Tennis

Cardio Tennis is popular with clubs and players. Courses offer how to teach Cardio Tennis classes, and certifications are given for completing these courses.

The primary goal with these classes is to keep your heart rate up. Always keep moving! These are good for players who want to exercise but have limited time in their busy schedule.

I've never taken one. The problem I have with Cardio Tennis is this: It's hard for me to watch people make the same mistakes and not correct their strokes or grips.

I've viewed these classes and I cringe watching people volley with the wrong grip and stroke production with certain shots. There isn't a consequence for making the same mistake. In this format, the pro doesn't feel the need to correct the players mistakes. Maybe I'm wrong in my assessment.

Most clubs will charge $20-$30 per hour and a half. The pro will probably make 70% of the total fees collected.

Club Mixers

Club mixers and tournaments can be a good revenue generator. Mixed doubles with couples either playing together or with someone is great for networking or socializing. Some events occur with either lunch or dinner may be included. Friday nights are popular at most clubs. This could be good for the club as well as the food and beverage manager.

Some people join a club to socialize. Other events that are popular are club championships. Mother-daughter, Father-son. Member-guest could expose others to a club they're not familiar with.

Pickleball

Pickleball is a sport that is on the rise. Some tennis clubs are turning tennis courts into Pickleball courts. The staff may have taped lines down or redo the courts into Pickleball courts.

I'm not sure what Pickleball is. I've watched it at clubs which changed their courts. I hate anything that takes away tennis players. This sport in my opinion is for a tennis player whose movement has diminished.

How do we exist with Pickleball? The tennis world always changes, and we must change. When you have a court with four tennis players on it and a court with 16 Pickleball players, from a club standpoint, the revenue difference with 16 vs 4 players is substantial.

What's the answer? We need to embrace it. Some friends who are pros don't like Pickleball, but they see it as a money-maker.

A friend had a Pickleball event that sold out with 40 players and dinner was included with a lesson. This was a two-hour event. The tennis tournament the prior week only drew 30 players.

I remember when the first Prince racquet came out. Traditional tennis players thought the racquet was cheating. That is, until they were beat by one. Pickleball reminds me of that feeling. This sport isn't going away.

Chapter 12
My Favorite: Tennis Parents

Quick Fix, Monthly Goals

THIS IS A unique chapter. Without parents, there wouldn't be students. Parents want the best for their kids. We all agree on that.

My concern is how they go about it. As a teaching pro, you are most likely to be the flavor-of-the-month. Meaning you're expendable; not always, but often.

Let's say you have a player who has been beating a lot of the same players in tournaments again and again. Then one day, that player loses to someone they've never lost to.

Sometimes the players' parents will inquire about the current coach of their opponent. That player just beat someone they've never beaten before. Often, the coach will get much of the praise even though it's one win.

Parents think there's a silver bullet, but if there is a quick fix, I don't know what it is. The parents don't understand that this is a long process and they want to see results.

As pros, we don't always get the point across

that it takes time. How much time? It's difficult to give up complete control to the pro. What is the time frame to develop a player? It doesn't exist. Parents can be frustrated, especially if that player is struggling in tournaments. Parents want to see results.

I try to plan three-month goals. For example, I was working with a 12-year-old girl. When we started, she was ranked around 270 in Southern California in the girls 12 & under singles. Three months later she was around 150. Three months later, around 75. Another 3 months inside the top 30. Four months later inside the top 5.

Three months at a time are attainable goals. You're working hand in hand with the parents and player. The outcome may not always be this good.

Most kids in the top 30 in their age group in Southern California are home-schooled. A typical day would be something like this:

- Starting at 6:30 AM comprises a personal trainer
- From 8:00-10:00 AM, personal instructions.
- Online home school from 11:00-2:00.
- From 2:30-4:00 PM, practicing with college hitting partners.
- From 6:00-7:30 PM a practice match with another junior or an adult.

That is a long drawn out day—grueling for a young child. This differs completely from 20 years ago. Kids were not home-schooled 20 years ago. It's like a job to be a great player. Long hours of training daily can be tiring.

Some kids and parents are delusional about their dreams. Yet, you never want to discourage any player about their dreams if the pro tour doesn't work out.

College Tennis

Most parents think their child will play Division 1 college tennis. Have you looked at a Division 1 college roster lately?

The rosters are mostly foreign players. I may know the reason.

Coaches like players who are independent. A player from France plays in a tournament in Germany. Technically, it's an international tournament. From a driving standpoint, it's similar to driving from Los Angeles to San Diego.

From a coach's standpoint, a player has international experience even though it's a relatively short drive. This player is speaking a different language in a foreign country. This makes the player more mature.

The most important thing a college coach will not tell you is this: The parents are not around which is less of a headache for the coach. These parents are still back in their home country. Therefore, numerous foreigners play college tennis. This is my opinion.

Some kids will not achieve a Division 1 college tennis scholarship. That realization is heartbreaking for some. I don't want to diminish anyone's dreams. Without dreams, what does anyone have to look forward to?

Numerous scholarships at Division 2 schools are available. NAIA is a good option. NAIA schools have plenty of good programs. Every tournament player should aspire to a free and partial scholarship for a college education.

Parents need to look in the mirror and understand how difficult college tennis can be.

Hitting Partners

Another intriguing idea has taken place the last few years: Hitting partners. What is a hitting partner, and how much are they paid?

This is an interesting story of a top 10 and under boy playing with a top 14 and under boy. Both were from Southern California. The parent of the 10-year-old boy would pay the 14 and under boy $40 for two sets. But for every game the 14-year-old boy lost they would deduct $2 per game, from the total of $40

If the 14-year-old lost 3 games, he would only get $34. The parent of the 10 and under who was paying, knew the 14-year-old was playing as hard as he could, or it would cost him money out of his own pocket.

Often, a better player or hitting partner tries to make that player they're playing with look good and miss a few balls to impress the parents.

Here is another experience I've had. Many parents think it's important to play with people better than you. I disagree. They need to play with players above and below their levels. They know they will have difficulty winning against the players above their level. Players may feel good winning two or three games. That's not how one should think about playing a match, winning two or three games is a good day.

Playing players your own level is important because you could win or lose. Playing a player below is important, because it teaches you how to win.

When you're playing someone above your level, you can remember what you did against a player below your level. That can translate into winning against a player at any level.

Here's another one. I have a great player at the 12 and under level. Her parents have hired college kids to play with her. The college player is getting paid $60 to play a few sets. The 12-year-old will never win and will not learn how to win playing a player at their own level because the kid hasn't won against the college level player.

This is good if you don't have a lot of players in your area to play with. The best advice is when you're playing a tournament. Parents are right next to you watching their kids playing their matches.

Some parents are nice and want to meet other parents and potential partners for their kids to practice with. This can be helpful in finding practice matches. Remember, they're giving up their weekends to play a tournament. They're serious about playing and improving like you.

One of the most important lessons I've learned was from a sectional champion. The fellow was unusual as a player and unique as a person. He was a member of the best tennis club in town and could play anywhere in town he wanted.

The champion agreed to a practice match with me, although he was much better than I was. I asked him if we could play at his famous tennis club.

"No," he said. "We'll play at this park with eight courts and no court dividers."

Balls rolled on our court frequently. Besides that, these courts were very quick. The courts were not well maintained. The surface was ground down and fast and combining that with balls rolling onto our court was distracting.

Behind the courts, the zoo with the train cruised by every fifteen minutes, the train whistle blowing. Every zoo has a monkey cage and the monkeys made monkey noises loudly.

To add to the confusion, a greenhouse lay as a backdrop. Greenhouses are a pale white color. The balls would blend in with the pale white color. It would be tough to pick up the balls coming out of the greenhouse backdrop. Most backdrops or windscreens are black or a dark green, which makes it easier to pick up a ball.

We played. I was going crazy with all the distractions. I was thinking, "What in the world am I doing at this place?"

Then my friend said, "We could play anywhere but if you practice and play here, you could play anywhere."

He was right. My advice is to play often at places with unusual surroundings. It will benefit you when you're back at your home court.

The average player does not enjoy getting out of one's comfort zone. It could be the speed of the courts, a playground nearby with crying kids, and people walking back and forth between the courts. Perhaps the courts are near to some train tracks and a busy highway with cars passing by.

Another good idea is to find courts without a windscreen or court dividers. This will help you focus on watching the ball coming to you without a dark background. Harder to see the ball. I know it doesn't sound difficult, but once you play without windscreens and then you play with windscreens, you'll see the difference.

When I first started out at a club in Colorado, we had one of the best junior tournaments I'd ever participated in. The main theme was that no parents were allowed to watch their kids play.

It was amazing. Kids ranked very high in their divisions. Adversaries suddenly became friends and found out they had much in common with their opponents.

After the matches, the kids moved into the pool party. Players who'd been trying to beat each other now swam together in the pool. Amazing to watch. For me, this is about opponents coming together and realizing they have more in common besides playing a sport.

Once the parents were allowed in to pick up their kids, most forgot it was a high-level JR tournament. They dropped the kids off several hours ago to win this tournament. Now, they were exchanging phone numbers and scheduling practice matches together. Now they are friends. Even parents who were adversaries broke the ice and now visited with other parents like long-lost friends. I learned much about human behavior during that junior tournament.

We could never get away with having a junior tournament without parents being allowed to attend.

NOTES

Chapter 13

Students Who Leave for Another Pro

Students Paying You

COACHES WHO LOST players for another coach can devastate a pro. This is like a breakup of a marriage. Some feel worse than that. I know one pro who stalked his former player until the police were involved.

Remember, the student is paying you. There is no contract. You're providing a service a player can cancel anytime.

You may have gone out of your way to help, going to tournaments, deals on lessons, a ride home. Free stringing of their racquets. A myriad of events can be possible. This happens all the time; students will come and go.

I've lost some and gained some. I learned a long time ago to avoid being attached to a player. Of course, I'm closer to some players than others. It still hurts when you lose them. That can get to you because it's part of the tennis business.

I've coached a high school team for some time and I work as a Director of Tennis at a country club.

It's hard for me to promote teaching at my club for my high school players. I may want them to take lessons from me, but I must be careful. It's a fine line. If they take lessons, would the parents think that a student might have a leg up on making the team?

But what is hurtful is they are aware I'm the pro at the country club. Some will go to a competitor. That's their right to do whatever they want, but you'd like them to stay with you. It can be hard to promote your business.

This is where you learn that this is a tough part of the business. The sooner you learn this, the easier it will be, and better for your ego.

Chapter 14
Social Media

Facebook and Instagram

SOCIAL MEDIA IS a necessary evil. Twenty years ago, we hadn't yet known about Facebook, Instagram, Tumblr, and others. When I started working, it was word of mouth about good pros. If a pro wasn't good, the student didn't come back for another lesson.

Now, social media often drives lessons for pros. Facebook and Instagram may be the focus of the main advertising for lessons.

Instagram is popular among pros and young people. I don't have an Instagram account. Some of my friends who are directors of tennis swear by this, that it is part of their marketing program.

Pros post events on their social media sites, adding pictures of their players and students. Parents react by thinking the pro must be a great pro because the players' pictures are featured on their site.

Parents are as guilty as the pros. They let them use their child's pictures. The player attends one practice at a facility, and the pros show the player on their pro's home page. Just like that, their pictures and bios are everywhere on the pros' website.

That would be like shopping at Walmart one time and now you're their best customer. This is the way people currently behave. Frequently, parents new to the tennis business don't research the pros. Many parents determine that if the pros have good players shown on their social media pages, then they must be good.

Several tennis programs are shown on Facebook, Instagram, and others. If someone is posting pictures and getting "Likes" for those posts, often people think, "It's great!"

They may not be the greatest players or teachers, but they're winning at social media.

A friend of mine who has a big name, played on the tour, and was a college NCAA team champion once said, "We're great pros but we're getting beat 6-0, 6-0 in social media every day for not doing what some of these other pros do on social media."

I'm older and I'm proactive to becoming more social media savvy. Don't get stuck in the old ways. Learn from my mistakes and get involved with social media.

Tennis Apps

If you're a pro, this could be another way to increase your income. Tennis apps are connecting players with one another. Players can find pros and lessons through these new apps. Meet-up groups are popular. Tennis apps for phone and tablets are everywhere.

This is where people can sign up for tournaments, search for events, find rankings and lessons.

There are some that have pro players rankings, bio and tournament updates. You can also buy equipment through an app. All the grand slams have apps for their draws, players bios, and schedules for the following day.

There's an app that connects players together for matches and flex leagues. It's called the *Tennis Pal app*. Check it out. It's terrific!

Websites and Getting Your Work Published

A good website is crucial. You can design your own website. Website designers cost much less now than five years ago.

Clubs' websites feature their pros' backgrounds. Everyone has his or her own bio, and each has a list of lessons and groups, plus prices.

If you have your bio on the club's website what makes you different and sets you apart from other pros?

On your bio, you could mention a suggestion about community service. Once a week give a lesson to underprivileged kids. Volunteer for an after-school program. Help kids with disabilities.

I did a clinic for the March of Dimes and it was one of the most fulfilling things I've ever done. The looks on these kids' faces were pure joy! If they don't have courts, bring a small net with low compression balls.

The USTA Net Generation sent me a bag with 20 junior racquets plus two dozen red & yellow balls. Their mission is to grow the game. You might start an after-school program. Your generosity by giving away a few lessons or two would be appreciated.

The San Bernardino shootings occurred a few

years ago. I put together a clinic that benefited the United Way. We raised a fair amount of money. There was coverage of information that appeared on Facebook, Instagram and other social media platforms. Regional newspapers and radios featured interviews.

It was great giving back and helping others. It was one of the most gratifying things I had ever done. When you give back, you'll get so much in return.

Years ago, I received a letter about publishing a tennis tip. I was bored one day, so I sent in a tip. The tip was on a slice approach shot. My tip was hitting the slice approach shot in the shape of a banana.

The tip was a good one. Everyone can relate to the shape of a banana. The ball stayed low forcing that player to hit up and the next shot would be an easy volley. I sent the tip to *World Tennis Magazine,* which is now out of business. When I sent in the tip, I had to sign a disclaimer asserting that if they used it I couldn't make any profit. I thought nothing more about it.

I was on my way to the LA Open at UCLA. I stopped at my Post Office mailbox and I thumbed through *World Tennis Magazine.* In the top 100 tips, there was my tip!

I believe it was 1988. The USPTA also published the tip in the *USPTA ADDvantage Magazine.* I found out they published it by sheer luck.

A friend who was a member of the USPTA told me about it. The USPTA may have published it many more times, but I'll never know. It could have been an instructional video. I'll be honest with you, that tip I took from someone else's who was another pro. I'm sure they in turn took it from someone else before them.

Other pro friends have written tips in this booklet. I believe they called it "Best 100 Tips" and it was available for sale. I don't know that they received any compensation or if it was just good getting their name recognition in that format. I'm sure pros would like to have their name attached to an established publication.

Numerous publications are helpful. One is a monthly publication *Tennis Industry* magazine which is an USPTA publication. This is a great magazine with many tips and information on stringing, running pro shops, retail sales, and other ideas.

Some websites show terrific information about the pro tour. One of my favorite websites is *www.tennisthis.com*. This person's site is a good friend. He's one of the most knowledgeable people in the tennis business.

Many racquet and ball companies use their own apps. You can purchase products and see which pros are affiliated with these products.

If I didn't have a website, I might not have reconnected with someone after 32 years. This is a book about the tennis business, but my website changed my life when this person reached out to me after such a long time. All I can say is that one email from my website changed my life.

As you can tell, websites are great for information about your program. The new USTA *Net Generation* is advertising's my program which is nice. Having someone build your website is much cheaper than it was say five years ago. I was fortunate with mine. I found a starving college student who was majoring in website design. She needed someone to build a site for in one of her classes at school. It was a great deal for me.

This could be an opportunity with college students for your websites. Another good site for something like this is this site called *Upwork.com*.

Many high school kids can now help with websites. Remember, many high schools now use an iPad instead of books. These kids are way ahead of you and I in computer skills and technology.

On a lighter note, please see the *Tennis Police* video on YouTube, it's hilarious!

Chapter 15
Pros With No Morals

PROS WITH NO morals: Where do I start?

Supposed a person visits a public park or a high school tennis court. The court isn't reserved yet there is someone teaching a lesson with a basket of balls. The pro most likely isn't USPTA-PTR certified. If an injury occurs, what happens?

No one thinks about that. Then the public is waiting for the court wondering why there is a lesson on the court without a sign on a gate. This could happen every day. How do you fix this? Most people taking a lesson couldn't care less. They want to improve their tennis game.

How can pros schedule lessons without a court reservation? This is a grey area in the tennis business. We've all been guilty of this. The first tennis lesson you ever teach is probably on a public court somewhere. You're young and able to make a few bucks. Somebody wanting to buy a few lessons for their kids and spend less money. I was guilty of this in the beginning when I started.

Some pros don't reserve the courts and have no contracts for court reservations. This is the dark side of being a teaching pro.

If you're a student, ask the pro what kind of insurance they have. Are you a pro if you go on the court with the basket of balls? Do you need a certificate, and do you need a background check? You should, but many pros are out on a court with the basket of balls and teaching a lesson.

Is that right? No, but it happens often. How do we fix that? Should you be a USPTA pro to be on a public court? Is it the duty of the students to find out what the background of the pro is?

I've seen pros while you're teaching a lesson, they'll put flyers on your student's windshield advertising while you're teaching the student. Is this immoral? Yes, it is, but it happens frequently.

How do we get rid of these people in the tennis business? Are we afraid of them? Should we be allowing that behavior to continue? The only way this will stop is if communities and Parks and Recreation police their tennis court. Most do not have the staff to do this. It's highly unlikely it will stop. That's why it continues to this day.

The only way this will stop is to convince parents and players to talk to the city. Local players tell the city that their courts are being used for lessons. An accident most likely on those courts would close down the court or taken out for Pickleball!

I've seen pros contact players' parents they see at tournaments. Pros walk up to parents and let them know their pro is not teaching this student the right way. Most parents will listen to this pro, especially if that pro has developed a few good players.

Occasionally, a pro tries to solicit their services to another parent. This is disgusting, even though they know that a parent's child is with some other pro. Many pros will speak badly of other pros behind their back. I can't tell you how many times

I've heard other pros speak ill of another pro. I've been around big names who badmouth other pros.

Sexual Misconduct

The next topic would be sexual misconduct between a pro and their students. I've known several pros and coaches' careers and their lives destroyed because of misconduct. Some have gone to prison because of their misguided behavior.

The sexual misconduct narrative has changed in the last few years. Look at all the Hollywood actresses and women who have come forward. The Me Too movement has taken off. It took a lot for these individuals to come forward. Accusations are taken seriously by clubs, schools, and cities.

My advice after coaching women's college and a girls' high school team is this: Avoid being alone with girls for any length of time, especially if you're male. I know it doesn't sound right. You're trying to be a coach and a friend. It's the only way to avoid these potential problems.

Young kids are impressionable and some look for attention. What better way to get attention than accusing the coach of improprieties. If you're accused, it can be very difficult to get rid of these accusations. Many will be suspended indefinitely with no form of proof. This is tough for sure!

Coaches Who Change Schools

Coaches who change schools often. I knew a high school coach who coached at four different high schools. I asked about each school he coached at and why he left. The first reason, they didn't pay enough. Okay, fair enough. The second one, left for a better situation. I wasn't sure what that meant? The third reason, it was time. Time for what? I heard they hired him for the fourth job because he was a good coach. I'm thinking four different jobs is too many for a high school.

It also says what morals do schools have to hire a coach who has been all over the place? Do they want to win at any cost? My answer is yes, they do. Some athletic directors have tremendous pressure on them from the school to win. Remember: student first, the athlete second? Does that value still hold true?

Numerous schools support good quality morals. How do you find out which programs want to win at any cost? You'll find out by word of mouth and the turnover at that facility. The stable facilities are out there. Look at the leadership at the top, from tennis director or head coach down to the assistants.

How long has that facility had a good program? So much of the tennis business is common sense and doing the right thing. If you continue to take the high road instead of going behind someone's back, you'll be ahead in this business. Once again, it's common sense

Here's another story that is unbelievable. I was working at my club when I was approached by a girl and her parents. We talked about taking lessons from me. She would be a freshman in high school. We worked together for three years and I became good friends with her and her family.

When it was time for her senior year, her coach at the high school retired. She then asked me if I wanted the coaching position.

I thought to myself, "Do I want to coach a high

school team, after many years before coaching NAIA and Division 1 college tennis?"

I'd never coached high school, and I always told myself I would not do that again. However, I did. The reason I took the position was because of her and her family. It was also her last year of high school.

But before I started, there was some unfinished business. A so-called pro was using the high school courts for his own lessons. Some of my students would sometimes go to his workouts. Then they would come back and tell me this guy was telling them how bad I was. I'd never even meet this guy before and he says bad things about me. I told the school before I ever worked there that he had to leave.

They gave him till September, and he still showed up. Then, October he remained there. The parents were frustrated. The school had not insisted on the ultimatums to leave. I kept telling them I'm not going to be employed there till he's gone. Yet he wouldn't leave. The school finally changed the locks on the courts, and at last he left.

There's more to the story but I'm sure you can fill in the blanks. I've heard many stories about this and how unique he was to other pros.

NOTES

Chapter 16
Racquet Stringing

USRSA

RACQUET STRINGING IS vital to becoming a good pro. Set yourself apart from the other stringers and become a certified racquet technician through the United States Racquet Stringing Association (USRSA).

A pro must be knowledgeable about strings, equipment, and playability.

Strings

Strings are a choice of the player. I love certain strings and find others are stiff and lack playability. Strings changed and improved so much in the last 10 years. They are made from different new materials. I suggest learning about hybrid stringing. Learn about the characteristics of Polyester, Co-Poly synthetic, gut, and various string tensions. Most string companies post string playability and string tension suggestions on their websites.

A racquet technician sounds impressive. I've strung racquets for over 40 years. I've educated myself on polyester and Co-poly strings, tensions, etc. But the industry constantly changes with new strings.

String companies are keen to sell strings at wholesale. They're aggressive in pricing. The companies may offer a special buy of two reels and get a third reel free. Most companies are great about free samples. It doesn't hurt to ask.

Buying strings buy the reel can make a profit for you. Let's say the cost of a set of strings from a reel is $4-$6. Not sure how much your labor is worth to you? Everyone is different. Suppose you charge $30. You've made $20 to $25 minus your labor. Is it possible you could string 3-5 racquets a day? You can see the potential of income.

I wish I had completed and taken the certification for the United States Racquet Stringing Association (USRSA). The Association provides newsletters about strings and stringing patterns. Friends of mine that are certified are very knowledgeable about stringing.

Equipment

If you want a stringing machine, you don't have to buy a new one. I have an old Ectolan stringing machine that's over 30 years old. I use a calibrator after every string job. It takes five minutes.

Electric stringing machines are the most modern stringing machine. They're accurate. I've never strung on one. As mentioned, I've used an old Ectolan for years. It may not be the most current machine, but I know what 50 pounds feels like.

I've learned from friends who played on the tour. Pros who had their racquets strung at ATP events take their own strings on tour. They also brought a calibrator to use on the stringing machine before they strung the racquet. They could feel if it was a pound or two off.

Clamps are a major part of stringing. If the strings slip through the clamps, there will be a loss of tension. I'm not sure how much tension is lost, but it will not be accurate on the number of pounds on the racquet.

Drop weight table top models are a good introductory machine. These are efficient for learning how to a string. Some stringers love these, but I prefer a standalone stringer to a tabletop model. Desktop stringers are easy to store and relatively inexpensive for stringers to learn on.

Learning to String

When I started, I strung a lot of gut. The tensions were higher, plus racquets were mostly wood racquets. I haven't strung gut in a long time. I'm curious to see what improvements have been made in the durability of gut. I'm sure most stringers have strung little gut.

I remember the first racquet I ever strung was the blue head racquet.

My first-string job was stringing with gut. I must have broken the gut three or four times. The grommets back then were awful. Cheap plastic with rough edges. They would nick the gut string whenever you pulled the string through the grommets.

By the end of stringing this racquet, I had made a mess of it. I had to use another set of gut to finish the string job. I'm sure we lost money and my boss wasn't happy with the outcome. But in time, I learned.

I find it helpful to write every string job date and tension down for my clients. When they come back, they can tell me what they like and how long since their racquet was strung.

To learn to be a superb stringer, it takes a lot of racquets and trial and error. If you don't know how to string, pay someone to help teach you. Does YouTube have lessons on stringing? I'm sure they do.

Contact local high school coaches to start your business. Most of the time they know a little about stringing or where to go for stringing. Put flyers in clubs and parks.

Discover as much about strings as possible. There are so many brands and different tensions. Learn to string and regrip racquets. Doing this will help establish your stringing business.

Chapter 17
Interviewing Process

What Clubs or Facilities Want to Hear

WHEN A CLUB or public facility needs to interview a new candidate for a job opening, this process is not enjoyed by most employers in the tennis business. My experience tells me employers want someone who hasn't moved from facility to facility. They want someone who is stable.

Sometimes to build a resume the person must move or relocate to another job. My suggestion is to stay at the same facility if possible. Employers want to hear that you live close to the facility. A long drive can cause a chance of car problems or transportation issues.

Interviews are difficult to arrange with a candidate who lives in another state. Employers would like the candidate to live in the same area.

USPTA & PTR Certifications

These days you must be a member of the United States Professional Tennis Association (USPTA), or the Professional Tennis Registry (PTR). Members are covered with insurance in case of an accident.

Employers want pros with insurance.

These two organizations have become import-ant in the last few years. It's impossible to hire you without being a member. Spend the money and get certified. You're going nowhere if you don't have the certification from one of these organizations. As far as the USPTA exam, many pros would go over the on-court testing with you. A review process is available for taking this test.

I'm less familiar with the PTR. If you are inter-viewing for a job, you do not need to talk about your playing background much. Instead, discuss what you've done in the tennis business, how you've related to people, and what you've done for the community.

What vision do you have for the Junior pro-gram? How would you get along with others? What would you do on the weekends? Would you be able to work most weekends?

That's what the employers want to hear. They want to count on you for those long days and long evenings. You'll be there doing tournament draws, helping with Junior programs, making phone calls, and being available for the members to hit with from time to time when they don't have another player to play with.

Let them know if you're affiliated with a special project. Is there a community program you could do for underprivileged children? You could make the club look favorable to the outside world. It's important to give back, even if players don't have the money for lessons. There's much you could do to allow these players access to lessons.

You could also volunteer for community ser-vices that involve the tennis facility. If it's a public facility, try to attend city council meetings. There is always time to get up and talk. It's important to attend parks and recreation meetings.

People love to hear about facilities and programs at these meetings. If you volunteer for these, there's not a club or facility that wouldn't want to hire you.

You'd do much of the clubs' public relations. Mention once a month having a free junior or an adult clinic for your facility. Help with the maintenance of facility, washing, and maintaining the courts. Make sure you're available for stringing. Clubs and facilities must have a reliable stringer. This is a plus and a good way to make extra income.

Most employers want references you've worked for, or still are working for. Most new jobs require two reference letters, and contact information. A background check is most likely, and possibly a live scan. They're simple to take. It's important to not burn any bridges in your past. These are sources you may need.

Another thing that is never mentioned, but is prevalent, is age discrimination. Hiring pros over the age of 60 is disappearing quickly. Think about this one.

I'm sure everybody knows a great pro over 60 with an unbelievable background and resume. This might be someone who has mentored players. Maybe the pro has health issues or cannot be on the court for over three hours at a time. Do clubs or facilities want to hire someone at this age? I don't know of too many facilities that would. Nevertheless, these pros are reliable and their wealth of knowledge of the game is unsurpassed.

I knew of a pro here with an enormousness big

name who was let go. This was three years ago, and he still hasn't found another position. Surely, it has something to do with his age. Hopefully you'll think I'm wrong about this and hopefully I am. Just look around you.

Chapter 18

Facility, Maintenance, and Appearance

First Impression

THE FIRST IMPRESSION of a tennis facility will be etched in one's mind like a photograph. I remember going often to tennis clubs over the years. Older clubs stand out because of their quaintness. Denver Tennis Club and LA Tennis Club are in expensive localities. Trees and beautiful homes enhance the neighborhood. Most tennis players will never experience these areas.

For the rest of us, it's a public facility or a club. I first notice whether the facility courts are well maintained and washed. Most successful clubs wash their courts once per week. In contrast, cleaning is difficult for a park or a public facility. Water restrictions can hamper cleaning, plus available staff to help. Often, the pros are the ones who do much of the maintenance.

Lesson Balls

Next is lesson balls, I've been guilty of having

poor lessons balls. It's possible to order balls from the retailers. The shipping cost can vary from different suppliers. My favorite way of providing balls is from tournaments.

They won't have over two sets on them. Tournaments will sometimes sell a can of tournament balls for $1 per can. Walmart and Costco have good deals on balls. In my experience, sales reps are not excited about selling balls. Profit is low, and shipping is a headache and costly.

If you're fortunate to have a ball machine, some of the poorest balls may be good ball machine balls. Spend more money on balls to set yourself apart. Students will come back even if you're not the greatest teacher. But good quality balls will be a good step forward.

Some clubs leave ball hoppers and ball mowers on the court. Mowers are awkward to store and move. Personally, I believe ball mowers should be put away when not in use. This equipment is one more thing to trip over when running for a ball.

Net Maintenance

Nets are a priority. In California, the top of the net is made of plastic which degrades from the sun and heat. The net itself is fine, but the top of the net is destroyed. It's frustrating.

Sometimes I've used zip ties to hold it together. It's a "band aid," but it works. There is an answer for trying to get a new net for your facility. The net is a good device to pull behind a tractor on a golf course to rake the grass. It also works on a baseball infield.

Sometimes selling it that way to the school or

the club will work. Most facilities will not think the nets need replaced perhaps due to lack of money in the budget.

Windscreens, Water Broom, Lights

Windscreens are vital to keep dirt and trash off the courts. The visual look of washed clean windscreens is wonderful. It keeps the club looking sharp and can set the tone when walking through the club's door. I wish there were a simple way to show the importance of windscreens.

Some facilities don't have windscreens, or windscreens are taken down due to severe winter weather. When possible washing the courts, the staff could use a hose for washing the windscreens like washing the side of a house. It makes such a difference.

Water brooms are a must for washing courts. They are simple to use, like vacuuming a floor. Washing a tennis court can become a tedious task. A person must help dragging the hose around. If someone does not pick up the hose on the court, a big line of dirt will lie under the hose. Sometimes it looks worse than when you started.

When washing the court, is water left standing around the courts? Our golf course has major run-off from watering. It's a headache. A good relationship with the grounds crew superintendent is vital. Buy a good water broom designed for washing the courts. A good one will cost $150-$250.

If you're lucky enough to have lighted courts at your facility, that's terrific. However, sadly lights can be difficult to replace. Most facilities will rent a lift device to rise to the level of the lights. Occasionally, the lift device will not fit thru the gate. Some of the fence may be disassembled. This could be time consuming and costly if renting the lift.

LED lights have made tremendous progress in saving electricity. They're much brighter and more efficient. Consequently, this is an expensive repair. Most lights were likely installed when the courts were built.

My advice is to replace as many bulbs as possible at the same time. Try, if possible, to write the date you replaced the lights and average hours the lights are operating. You may determine how many hours the bulbs may last and estimate your budget for future repairs.

Squeegees are important to use after rain or washing the courts. Keeping the squeegees maintained by hanging them upon the fence will extend the life. Never leave the squeegees on the court. The squeegee roller will be flat spotted and can be ruined.

It's important to check the net height daily. Center straps can fray and break. Benches, tables, and chairs and on-court furniture can add a tremendous amount of ambiance. If you arrange to remove patio furniture when the weather is bad, it will last longer. It's not always easy to do.

A nice touch to your club is score cards. Players love score cards on the court.

I noticed one problem at my club. Sprinklers can spray water from the golf course onto the windscreens. This can create dirt on the court and leave a huge black stain. How do we fix this? If your club is like mine, tennis isn't important. It's all about golf. which pays most of the bills.

Tree limbs hanging over the fence on the courts are another problem. Beside leaves, trees have little berries that fall on the court and players step on them and squish the berries, leaving a stain. Sometimes the wind will blow the berries and leaves off. This is a huge headache for court cleaning.

The stains with berries, water from the golf course, and the dirt from the windscreens are headaches.

Trash cans might hang on the net posts. They become an eyesore when full of plastic tennis cans and bottles. Who empties that, you or the maintenance crew? My experience is that I would empty them to avoid confusion.

NOTES

Conclusion

MY EXPERIENCES COVER 45 years in the tennis business. I'm sure I can't remember or have forgotten a few stories, and I imagine I'll remember them after I finish this book. Isn't that how it always is?

I hope you enjoyed reading the book as much as I did writing it. It brought back a lot of stories and memories I'd forgotten about.

Lots of lessons learned the hard way in this business.

Hopefully there are some things that may have inspired you in this book.

I believe this: You can always learn from others. Somebody out there is ready to start a tennis career. That person too could have a book to write about their experiences one day. Who knows? If I could inspire one person from this book, it will be worth it.

I didn't write this book to profit. If I sell one book, I will be thrilled because I have a story to tell. Everyone has one book ready to come out. This is my one book.

The tennis business has been fantastic. Many of my closest friends I've met are from tennis. I always felt it was my mission to grow the game of tennis.

A wonderful healthy lifestyle has kept me healthy all these years. My goal is to be an ambassador for the sport. You must be the judge. So many of my friends are still competing in tournaments well into their late 60s and 70s. I see my doctor for a checkup every six months. He says tennis is keeping me alive and healthy. How many doctors will tell you that? Many, I hope.

❀ Good luck! ❀

Scott Smith

- Awarded 2013 USPTA District 5 Pro of the Year. Southern California.

- USPTA member since 1979.

- Wilson Advisory staff member since 1978.

- Director of Tennis Arrowhead Country Club, San Bernardino.

- Recently served on USTA Adult League Committee.

- Recently served on USTA grievance committees.

- Founder of Mountain Resorts USTA Jr. Satellite & Fast 4 Tournaments.

- Helped organize USTA Quick Start Program in seven elementary schools.

- Presently Girls and Boys Varsity High School Tennis Coach.

- Coached NAIA and NCAA Division 1 college tennis.

- Sectionals single rankings for 30 years in a row.

www.scottsmithtennis.com

Made in the USA
Middletown, DE
17 February 2022